If You Need A Minister
~ Wil Perkins ~
practical advice for hiring your next minister

21st Century Christian Publishing, Inc.

ISBN: 978-0-89098-491-8

©2013 by 21st Century Christian
2809 12th Ave S, Nashville, TN 37204
All rights reserved.

All rights reserved. No part of this publication may be reproduced, stored in a retrieval system, or transmitted in any form or by any means—electronic, mechanical, photocopy, recording, digital, or otherwise—without the written permission of the publisher.

Cover design by Jonathan Edelhuber

Contents

Introduction 7

Before You Begin 11

Who Are You? 19

Who Are You Looking For? 27

The Search Process 41

A Final Word 57

Sample Job Posting 60

Sample Interview Questions 64

Sample Work Agreement 66

Introduction

For one reason or another, you find yourself in need of hiring a new minister to fill the pulpit, proclaim God's Word to the flock, work with the youth, or assist you in a specific ministry. While you realize the decision is large, you may fail to understand how truly monumental it is. The minister you hire will have an impact on your church family, good or bad, which will last for years to come, even after he leaves. The decision you make today will determine the way your church grows in numbers and in faith. How do you begin to manage such an important process? What steps can you take to ensure the man is a good fit and not merely a good interviewee? These are questions that deserve a thoughtful answer, and it is just these questions that I will address on the following pages.

I have worked in ministry, both full and part-time, since 1988. I have gone on dozens of interviews and applied for hundreds of openings all across the nation. Sadly, the overriding characteristic I have experienced is a lack of organization and a defined objective in the search process by these churches. Since our congregations are autonomous, I wouldn't expect a standardized application. Yet, I am amazed at how many church leaders think that the procedure should be a simple three-step system. The first step is to determine they need someone; step two is to get the word out that they are looking; and step three is to hire the first candidate they like. Is it any wonder that we have such a high turnover rate among our ministerial staff, when we put so little thought and attention into finding a man who will work well with our congregations? While long tenure does not guarantee growth in churches, short tenures guarantee no growth and no stability.

I've also been on the other side of the coin and helped congregations looking for ministers. Because of this I understand the complexity of trying to find one person that fits well with so many different personalities. No candidate who interviews is going to be a perfect fit and any member can find something he/she does not like about an applicant or his family. In the end, if you try to please everyone, you end up pleasing no one.

My purpose for writing this book is not to set down a standardized process for congregations to use, but rather to spark discussions and thoughts on how we might improve the process, find better matches, and in the end, have to search for ministers much less often. My goal is to expose you to some ideas that will help you conduct the search for your next minister in a deliberate manner that will result in a good match for your individual congregation based upon more than an initial good impression.

PHASE

1
Before You Begin

Before beginning the search process, the leadership needs to work among itself as well as with the congregation to answer a few questions. The first question is why did the former minister leave? Was it voluntary or compulsory? If it was voluntary, what were his reasons for finding another position? Was it because there was a problem, was he looking for more money, or was he wanting to relocate to a specific area? Finding out why he left can help you discover if there are any issues the leadership needs to address before hiring a new minister.

This is a very critical first step. When it is not taken, the result may be having to deal with the same issues again, the minister possibly leaving, and you having to begin the search process all over again. This may place a great emotional toll on your congregation. This step is also very easy to gloss over; as it is rarely comfortable or easy to face internal divisions. Having your congregational issues in order before you begin the search is an imperative step to ensuring a healthy relationship with the next minister and his family.

If the minister's leaving was compulsory, what were the leadership's reasons for asking him to go? Was there a doctrinal issue, job performance concern, or personality problem? When there has been adversity between the leadership and preacher, these questions may be harder to answer. But once again, knowing and addressing these potential problems will help you to avoid the same mistakes when hiring your next minister.

Sometimes when a conflict arises within a congregation, the leadership assumes it can fix the problem by focusing on a single factor. This often results in the removal of the preacher or minister because there is a belief that a "fresh start" will automatically resolve the issue. However, conflicts tend to be more complex than a single issue, and removing the preacher may temporarily settle the problem, only to see it flare to life again at a later time. It would serve the church leadership well to dig a little deeper to seek out the root of the problem and solve it. Several of our universities offer mediation and conflict resolution specialists who can assist the leadership in uncovering and dealing with core problems.

Whether the minister left voluntarily or was let go, addressing the underlying issues will result in a healthier church and assist you in finding a more successful match with the next minister you hire. If his motivation had to do with issues beyond your control, there is probably little you can do to fix the problem. Understanding why you need to look for a new minister is critical before you even begin searching for someone to come in and work with you. Let me give a couple of examples to illustrate my point.

One congregation I worked with was dealing with troubles caused by the previous preacher, even though he had been gone for several years. The eldership decided to invite in a man who was a minister and counselor. He worked with a congregation on the other side of the state, thus minimizing his firsthand knowledge of anything that had transpired. Prior to his coming, members who had any issues were encouraged to anonymously set a time to speak with the gentleman by tearing off a time from a sign-up sheet, placing their name on the slip, and dropping it in a sealed box.

The man spoke to the congregation on Friday night about conflict and an assortment of ways to deal with it. Saturday morning he met with the various people who had signed up to talk to him. Saturday afternoon he had lunch with the elders and had them bring up any issues they felt were relevant. That evening he spoke to the entire leadership (elders, deacons, and minister) and their wives about internal issues the church was facing without revealing any of the names or specific circumstances. He brainstormed with us about possible solutions to these problems and provided simple tools to deal with them. Not everyone's problem was solved to their satisfaction, but knowing they had been heard and understood did a world of good for everyone's morale.

Another congregation I am familiar with was suffering through various problems. The eldership decided to "clean house" and fired the preacher and youth minister in order to get a "fresh start." After the selection process, a new preacher was hired and the problems returned. The elders decided to deal with the crisis in a three-step process. First, they got together, prayed, and decided to ask the congregation for their forgiveness for their previous lack of leadership, as well as ask for their continual support as they attempted to deal with the issues. Second, the entire eldership met with every member in his/her home and asked them to speak freely about whatever was troubling them. Finally, after meeting with everyone, the elders got together and determined what steps were going to be taken to solve the problems and announced them to the congregation. They made it plain that they understood that not everyone was going to be pleased, but they were, to the best of their ability, trying to deal with the issues and move forward. A few people started to complain again; but the elders quickly went to those individuals. They advised them that they were attempting to move beyond the problems. They were willing to work with them, but if they were going to keep stirring up trouble, perhaps they needed to consider worshiping at another congregation. This leadership allowed the body of believers to move forward, and they enjoyed a long relationship with their preacher.

Going through this process can be painful, but it can pay huge dividends in the form of a more peaceful congregation and, hopefully, a longer tenure of your ministerial staff. You might want to consider an interim preacher or setting up a rotation of speakers to fill the pulpit while you undergo this healing process. Before you begin searching, ask questions and solve any potential problems.

PHASE 2

Who Are You?

After dealing with any problems, you need to consider who you are as a congregation. Just as individuals have unique personalities and characteristics, a group can behave as an entity and possess character traits. In numerous places, the Apostle Paul refers to the church as a body that functions as a single unit. As with individuals, our personalities have both positive and negative traits. What makes us strong in one area may make us weak in another area.

In order to uncover your congregation's personality you may want to survey the membership and ask two simple questions: What is our greatest strength as a church? What is our greatest weakness? You may discover that the congregation has a generous spirit, but lacks the ability to connect to the community. Maybe you're a group that does a good job of making people feel comfortable, but fails to be strong on biblical truths. Understanding the congregation's strengths and weaknesses will help you make a better assessment of who would fit well with you in a long-term ministry relationship.

In your congregational profile don't forget the physical characteristics of your members and your community. Let's say you are an affluent congregation with a lot of professionals. You are going to want to hire a minister who can identify with your membership. I wouldn't recommend hiring a good old country boy even if he is a dynamic speaker and a charmer. The members of the congregation are going to want someone who can identify with their lifestyle at home and work and who will be able to address the spiritual problems they are experiencing. It's not that he couldn't do a good job for you, but you need to remember that you are looking for someone who is a good all around fit and will stay for a while.

Where your congregation is located (urban vs. rural) will affect who will be interested in moving to your area. If you are in a small, isolated community, make sure your candidate either has experience living this way or is aware of the limitations of your town. If a candidate has never lived in a community under 100,000, he might not be a good fit for you. This is not to say you can't have a successful relationship with someone who has never lived in a setting similar to your congregation; but you need to factor in the possible effect of the culture shock.

Being honest with yourself and your potential candidate about your location will save you both a lot of heartache and time. Just because you think your community and congregation are the greatest places in the world, doesn't mean that everyone will agree with you.

When looking at the physical characteristics of your congregation, also consider the age of your membership. If you are a congregation that is aging, you may tempted to hire a young man. But can he identify with your group? Some churches believe that if they hire a young preacher, he will attract younger members. It usually takes more than having a young face behind the pulpit to help a congregation grow. Youth can also mean a lack of experience and an influx of new ideas. An older membership may be reluctant to put up with on-the-job-training or changing the way they've always done things. Additionally, a young family will typically thrive in a congregation with other young families. It can place unnecessary stress on young parents when their children are the only children in the congregation. You may find yourself looking for a new preacher in a few years due to unavoidable conflicts.

It would also be wise for the leadership to determine in which direction they are going to lead the body of Christ. Let's say that you are a congregation and you want to attract new and younger members. Knowing which direction you wish to move as a body of believers will influence what man you want to hire to work with you toward that goal. You want a minister who has knowledge and/or experience in helping a church grow; but you are also making the commitment that you'll support and encourage him in this endeavor.

Let me tell you about Jack. He was a man in his early 60's who took his first preaching job at a small congregation in a Midwestern town of about 1,000 people. The church was comprised of mainly older members whose families had lived in the area for generations. Jack began his ministry with them by telling them everything they were doing wrong and how to fix it. Most of the membership, understandably, did not appreciate. He and his wife had spent most of their adult lives in a major urban area in Texas and were not accustomed to small town life. She was not shy about sharing her difficulty assimilating with others, constantly compared their old life to their new one. Jack continued to be frustrated in his work and felt he was banging his head against a brick wall. The town began to gossip about how the couple was not fitting into the community and the mounting problems at the church. Finally, everything reached a boiling point, and Jack and his wife quickly moved back to Texas.

This scenario is repeated in hundreds of congregations over and over again all because the leadership failed to determine who they were and who they wanted to become. Taking the time to understand who you are as a group and what direction you want to proceed will help guide your choice of who you want to hire to work with you.

PHASE 3

Who Are You Looking For?

The next step in the process is for the leadership to determine who they are looking for. I had an elder tell me once that he just wanted the preacher to get up every week, teach the truth, and to "marry 'em and bury 'em." I doubt that he really wanted something so simple, yet many congregations don't truly consider what they are looking for in their next minister. I would strongly encourage you to write down what the ideal preacher for your congregation would look like. Understand that an exact match to this person doesn't exist, but it provides you with a template to help you measure potential candidates. Here are some factors that you might want to consider:

Age and Experience

Sometimes I see ads that say something like, "We are looking for a minister between the ages of 35 and 45." The assumption is that maturity, wisdom, and experience come with age. This is not always the case. Some men don't even decide to pursue a career in ministry until later in life.

On the other hand, it is possible for someone in their late 20's to early 30's to have over ten years of experience working with congregations. Yet, this person would be disqualified from consideration because he wasn't old enough. The experience of the minister makes a big difference in how he is able to do his job. Consider how many years of experience you want your minister to have in addition to a possible target age- range.

Education and Skills

I once spoke with a woman who had visited another congregation and had heard a preacher give a lesson on the *Paraclete* (the Counselor, Comforter, Holy Spirit). She told me that she couldn't understand what a "parakeet" had to do with Jesus. I know men who are able to discuss the *Paraclete* or *paruousia* with the most knowledgeable scholars, but how does this knowledge help in their ability to work within a church?

I am incredibly indebted to our universities for my education. I have attended Freed-Hardeman University,

Harding School of Theology, Lipscomb University, and Abilene Christian University. My professors have shared a wealth of insight with me and helped me study and understand things I probably never would have on my own. This knowledge does the congregation I am working with little good unless I'm able to transform it into understandable terms for the average member of the congregation to digest and apply to their lives.

Most of the "Minister Wanted" ads I see are asking for potential candidates to possess some sort of degree in Bible. I believe in the power of a Christian education and having our young people exposed to professors who live and teach from a Christian worldview. While knowledge is valuable, you also want to consider what skill sets you want your minister to have. If during your congregational profile you discover that your members want the church to grow, you want someone who has the knowledge, but also the skills to help you accomplish this goal. Perhaps you discover that you are in need of a person who can counsel or who is an excellent teacher. You should look beyond book knowledge to real life skills.

In many ways the minister of a small congregation is like a small business owner. He needs to run the day-to-day affairs of the church, manage the office, do public relations, marketing, and fund-raising. Other skills you might want to consider include the ability to work independently or in a team structure, communicate with persons inside or outside the organization, critical thinking and problem-solving skills, ability to obtain and process information, being organized and able to prioritize work, able to analyze data, create and/or edit written reports, proficient with computers and software programs, being hardworking, confident, trustworthy, personable, disciplined, self-motivated, results-oriented, and reliable. Let me warn you again. The perfect fit doesn't exist. You'll need to determine what education and skills are essential and which would be nice for him to have, but are optional.

Independent and Team-player

I'll probably get in trouble for admitting this, but most preachers have fairly large egos. They think they can do it better than anyone else. As a result, some ministers do not play well with others. I had interviewed with a congregation for an Associate Minister's position several years ago. The preacher of that congregation invited me to breakfast on the Monday following my interview under the pretense of getting to know me better. After a few pleasantries, he informed me that there would never be a reason for me to ever be in *his* pulpit. He had been actively working behind the scenes to discourage anyone from being hired and he wasn't about to let anyone come in without letting him know his place.

Some congregations have multiple ministers or have an eldership that is very involved in the day-to-day operations of the church. If this is the case for you, you are looking for someone who can be a team player and isn't threatened by others who may share duties with him.

Other congregations expect their preacher to be self-motivated and "run the show." The leadership will step in if there is a problem; but otherwise, they expect the minister to be a go-getter. Knowing what type of leadership you expect from a minister will help you to seek out the person who will be the best fit for you.

Extroverts and Introverts

In the world of ministry, the extrovert is the "belle of the ball" and the introvert is often viewed as the ugly step-sister. On a human response level, it is easy to understand how we are attracted to charismatic, outgoing people. Nothing is as enjoyable as a speaker who fills you with "warm fuzzies." He is everybody's friend and the life of the party. Since an extrovert usually gets his batteries charged by being around people, a congregation with a lot of activities may be the perfect fit. In my experience, they are also the ones who are able to sway people to their way of thinking, whether its scriptural or not. While extroverts tend to make people happy, they also tend to overcommit. It's not that they didn't mean those promises when they made them, but they are predisposed to live in the moment and do and say what is necessary to keep people happy.

When I was between ministry jobs, my wife and I befriended the preacher at the congregation we were attending. We shared a lot of ministry related issues and he really looked after my family. He was the smiling, charismatic man we often think of as the typical preacher. I often noticed, while standing in line to shake his hand after the services, that while one person was talking to him, he was always scanning the crowd looking for the next person. He was rarely giving the person in front of him his full attention. After a few months I received a job offer that required us to move away. He gave a very sweet statement about how much we would be missed and how much we meant to him and to the church during our time there. Yet, he couldn't recall my wife's name, even though he repeatedly complimented her as the perfect preacher's wife. We weren't offended because we understood that, as an extrovert, he was much more concerned about giving "warm fuzzies" than recalling details.

Consider the introvert in comparison. He is not as outwardly charming or charismatic as your typical preacher, but he tends to be sincere, dependable, and trustworthy. If you ask him a question that he doesn't know offhand, he is more likely to admit it rather than trying to bluff you. He is willing to do research about it and come back with a thoughtful and possibly a more complete answer than what you wanted. When he visits he does not consider himself the center of attention and focuses on the person he is visiting. When he speaks to people, he gives them his undivided attention and seeks to truly know them as individuals. He also tends to be a deep thinker who can be counted on to be calm during a time of crisis. Obviously, you can't hire a *complete* introvert because churches need someone who can initiate conversations with people and is willing to spend time with others. Introverts can also appear to be emotionally distant from others. They tend not to openly exhibit feelings, which may leave some members feeling cold. Plus, introverts need down time away from people in order to recharge their batteries. These are my personal observations and by no means apply to each individual in every situation; but they are worth considering as you are looking for a minister.

Who's Ultimately Responsible?

In our discussion about leadership, we need to remember who is ultimately responsible for the health and well-being of the local congregation. Elderships are servant-leaders who are, in the end, responsible for what is taught in their congregations. They are to watch over the souls under their care and teach with sound doctrine so they can both exhort and refute when needed (Acts 20:28; Titus 1:9). Members of the congregation are to give these men the respect they deserve and submit to their leadership (1 Timothy 5:18-19; 1 Thessalonians 5:12-13; Hebrews 13:17). This includes any minister who works within the local body of believers. I'm amazed how many congregations are led astray by preachers who gain more influence than Scripture ever intended them to have and the elderships that allow them to get away with it. In the interview process, it is imperative that applicants understand that, while they have charge over a particular ministry, they do not have charge over the entire congregation.

Written Job Description

Before beginning the search process, write out a job description that includes specific tasks you expect the minister to accomplish, and what you as a congregation will do for him. Having this written down and signed by all parties involved protects everybody.

I know of a preacher who worked for a small congregation in the northeast. After he had been there for a while, people started to notice that he took a lot of time off and usually wasn't where they expected him to be during the week. When questioned about these irregularities, he said that when he was hired, the leadership had agreed to give him four weeks vacation. When questioned about his activities during the week, he said that he had never been told about office hours, a prison ministry, or doing a weekly devotional at the local nursing home. Enough time had passed that no one who had been involved in hiring him could remember what was or was not a part of their verbal agreement. If there had been a written job description that detailed his responsibilities and the compensation the congregation would provide, that document would have put everything to rest.

Please be realistic in coming up with your job description. I was interviewing with a group of elders and I asked them to tell me what they thought my job responsibilities as minister for that congregation would be. As we went around the room the men gave me the typical description of preaching, teaching, and visitation until we got to one man who told me that I should be at the beck and call of every member for anything they wanted or needed. This "hired servant" mentality is what drives men from the ministry, ruins marriages, and destroys families. One man cannot fill the needs and wants of an entire congregation without destroying his own life in the process.

Every work agreement I have had with an eldership always included the phrase, "and any tasks as assigned by the elders." A job description is a fluid document that can change with time. After working for several years with a congregation, the eldership decided that they wanted me to be involved in the local Bible camp. I sat down with them, we clarified the type of involvement that met their qualifications, and we wrote out a new job description which everyone signed. Everybody knew what was expected of me and what I needed to do to fulfill my obligations to them.

Be practical about the compensation package you are willing to offer to a man and his family. I talked with an elder once who told me that we need to keep the preacher poor so as to keep him humble. That may work well in theory, but in practice it is only going to cause strife in his family and prompt him to look for a better paying job after a few years.

For several years, the late Charles Siburt of Abilene Christian University conducted a minister's compensation survey by job classification, state, size of congregation, education, and experience level. This "Salary Survey" can provide you with examples of what other congregations are doing as far as pay, health insurance, retirement, and other compensations. Obviously, your unique circumstances need to be considered. A church shouldn't offer a man more salary than they can pay with the hopes he'll grow the congregation and expand the contribution before you run out of money. I also know of congregations that pay very little and yet have thousands of dollars sitting in a bank account for that proverbial "rainy day." If you want to attract the man who is going to do the best job, be a good fit, and stay for a long time, you're going to need to do your homework, especially if you want a man who has invested in an education.

When you draw up your job description, remember that the letters to Timothy and Titus are filled with Paul's instruction to these preachers (for a more detailed discussion see Everett Ferguson's work, *The Church of Christ*). In these letters Paul instructs that ministers not be quarrelsome, but be kind to everyone, able to teach patiently - even when wronged, correct people with gentleness, pursue righteousness, godliness, faith, love, endurance, and gentleness. Purity is a necessity in their lives as they are to be examples in speech, conduct, love and faith. He must be able to present the Word of God to others. We also see that he is to help organize the church (Titus 1:5), strengthen the faith of Christians, refute false teaching, and train others to carry on the work of the church.

PHASE 4

The Search Process

You have addressed any problems related to the last minister leaving, conducted a congregation and candidate profile. Now you are ready to begin searching for your next minister. This entire time you have been asking for God's wisdom and direction. Now, you will need to decide how the application process is going to work. Consider the following action steps.

Step One

Are you going to form a search committee or have the elders conduct the search? There are several advantages to the leadership appointing a search committee that is comprised of a cross section of the congregation. First, it permits members of the congregation to have a greater say in who is going to eventually be hired. This allows the membership to take personal ownership for the decision process. Second, the work of searching for a minister is spread out among the search committee rather than being placed on the shoulders of one or two people. The committee does the job of pre-screening the applicants before anyone is invited in for an interview. Third, it invites different perspectives on what the congregation is wanting from their next minister. This is especially true if the last minister's leaving was troublesome. Sometimes the relationship between the leadership and previous minister was so contentious that the search process is already fraught with problems. In other cases, the makeup of the congregation could have drastically changed since the hiring of the last minister and therefore the needs of the membership have changed as well.

Often the reason elderships are reluctant to hand over the search to a committee is because they fear the loss of control of the decision making process. However, this doesn't have to be a concern if the search committee is set up properly from the beginning. The eldership can give the group clear parameters when searching for potential candidates with the understanding that the final decision will be made by the elders. The committee chair can provide regular updates to the elders and/or one of the elders can serve on the committee.

Having a search committee made up of a cross section of the congregation has many more advantages than disadvantages. If you are going to form a search committee, studies in group dynamics conclude that groups work best with five to seven people. More than that and the process begins to break down.

Step Two

Decide what information you are going to want from the candidates. Usually congregations request a resume and copies of recent lessons. Depending on the criteria you have established, you may want to request other information such as bulletin articles, class material, or a philosophy of ministry statement.

Step Three

Consider how you want to advertise your opening. You have two options available to you: word of mouth or placing an announcement with one of the brotherhood publications or Christian schools. There are advantages and disadvantages to both. If you advertise, you will likely get several responses for every ad you place. The more widely you advertise, the more work the elders or the search committee will have to do in narrowing down the applicants. Also, *where* you advertise will affect what type of applicants you receive. Our universities and publications have various reputations as to where they are on the liberal to conservative scale. Don't assume that your *alma mater* has the same reputation it did when you graduated. Seek out advice from those who keep in the know about these things. If you choose to simply advertise by word of mouth, you can expect to get fewer applications, but they ought to be ones which should be a closer fit to what you are looking for.

Step Four

Consider how long you will accept applications. Having a cut-off period will help you narrow down your candidate pool and allow you to continue to move forward in your search process. Typically this is about thirty days. Allowing the application process to drag on indefinitely wears down the people who are conducting the search and discourages those who applied early. If anyone applies after the cut-off time, you can inform him that the filing date is past and thank him for his interest.

Step Five

Decide who is going to handle the applications as they come in. Assign a person to accept and acknowledge the receipt of the material sent to you. Communication is the key component of this step. It is easy to set up a free email account that is dedicated to receiving applications and responding to questions from candidates. I strongly encourage you to respond to everyone who applies and let him know that you have received his material. In your response, let him know how you have determined the process will work, and when he can expect to be contacted one way or the other. The standard rule of thumb is that if you have not heard from an employer in 60 to 90 days that you are no longer a serious candidate. I've had congregations get in touch with me over a year after I originally sent in my information, even though I haven't had any contact with them in the meantime. If a minister is interested in making a move, he is not going to sit around and hope to hear from one church. He is going to apply for multiple positions and, if you let the screening process go on indefinitely, he may already be hired by someone else.

Step Six

Review the applicants by applying your candidate profile to them. See if they have the education, skills, and qualifications you have already determined you are seeking. Those who fail to measure up should be contacted and informed that you are no longer considering them as potential candidates.

Step Seven

This is really important – do phone interviews. Have a set number of questions that you will ask every applicant. The elders or the search committee can set up a time to speak with the candidate. You can use a speaker phone or do a conference/video call so everyone can hear. The point of this interview is for you to ask specific questions to help you narrow down candidates that you will invite for a visit later. If there is a "hot button" topic for your congregation, the phone interview is the time to bring it up. These may be issues that are the subject of debate within the brotherhood. It is better to discuss these subjects over the phone rather than inviting an applicant in and finding out that you are completely incompatible in some critical area. This also allows the applicant to ask questions that may help him determine if he is truly interested in working with you.

Step Eight

Cut down your list to the top candidates and inform the rest that they are no longer being considered. Now is the time to check references and job histories. I've had search committees ask permission to do criminal background checks and review my credit score. Be aware that when checking with previous employers you are only getting one side of the story. Every minister I know has at least one horror story of how they and their family were treated at a particular congregation. If you uncover any questionable information, schedule another phone interview and ask the applicant to clarify any issues. Do not automatically discount a good applicant based on negative feedback from one individual or one situation.

I once worked with a congregation that had an eldership, but was run by a matriarch. She was the wife, mother, grandmother, aunt, and relative of ninety-nine percent of the congregation; and everyone did what she wanted. I had the misfortune of being involved in an incident that publicly embarrassed her. My work with the congregation was over at that point. However, since the congregation had a reputation of never firing their preachers, I wasn't let go. Instead, my family and I were ostracized. Members would talk to us as long as we were out of sight of the matriarch; but as soon as she entered the room, everyone would walk away from us. Other members of her family verbally attacked me and my family. I eventually resigned, and her family informed me that I would never get a job as a preacher in that area ever again. To this day, they have held on to their grudge. Take the time to seek out both sides of the story. If a minister has gone through a bad situation, he can usually provide a reference who will be more unbiased in recounting the facts.

You might also want to consider having a member (or two) of the search committee make an unannounced visit to his home congregation, if it is feasible. As a preacher, when I am invited to speak somewhere else I usually pull out my "Cadillac" sermon because I wanted to dazzle everyone with my brilliance. The truth is that the "try out" sermon might be nothing like his normal sermon. It gives you the opportunity to check him out as a teacher and a preacher. You'll be able to see how he relates to the congregation and pick up additional information from the members. It may also raise some red flags that you would have been unaware of otherwise. The inherent problem with the unannounced visit is that your candidate might not be there when you come; but it still gives you the opportunity to get a feel for his work as it is reflected in his congregation.

Step Nine

Plan the activities that you would like your potential minister to be involved in during his visit to your congregation. My family and I have traveled hundreds of miles just to entertain ourselves all day Saturday while we waited for the big event on Sunday. It left us with the impression that the congregation wasn't really prepared or interested in us as individuals.

Here are some suggestions to help you make the most of the visit. Have an informal get together on Saturday evening with members of the search committee or elders and their wives. This is a time to get to know the candidate and his family on a personal basis and possibly ask any follow-up questions. Sunday the applicant will give the requested lessons, have the formal interview with the elders, and meet the various members of the congregation. Be sensitive about his family's travel requirements. He may need to be back by Monday morning, especially if his spouse works and his children are in school. You may want to wrap things up early in the afternoon so they can begin their return trip.

Consider putting together an informational package about your community and taking them on a tour of your area. Investing time in your candidate lets you get to know them better and tells them that you care about them.

Let's take a moment and be honest about the interview process. We say that we are interviewing the man for the ministry position, but we almost always expect his family to come with him. They might not be a part of the formal interview, but everyone is checking them out. Take it easy on his wife and children. She may be his steel magnolia, but wilt under the constant glare and scrutiny you are giving her and her children. Please understand that she is being thrust into an awkward situation where people are evaluating her and her family and sometimes making a snap judgment. I've had women attempt to assess my wife as a potential friend, confidant, or rival in the few hours we've spent with their congregation.

Be realistic about what you expect of an applicant and his family when they visit you. They may have traveled for hundreds of miles to come to a place where they are all on show and it creates a stressful environment. While this cannot be helped, build in time for the family to be alone and talk privately about their impressions of you. We went on an interview once where the congregation requested we show up Friday afternoon. They had something scheduled Friday night, and several events on Saturday and Sunday. After keeping us running the entire time, by Sunday night we were completely wiped out. One of the members of the search committee noticed our haggard state and quipped that they had taken it too easy on us. Remember, you are looking for someone to work with you, but they are looking for a home, a place for all of them to belong.

Step Ten

Once you have planned the activities you want to include in their visit, you are ready to have your final candidates come to a visit. You have two options as to how you want to handle this process.

• **Option 1** is the more traditional way to finalize your decision. You invite your top three candidates to come in for a visit on consecutive weekends or as close together as possible. The advantage of this option is that it allows the members to be able to compare applicants before too much time has passed. When seeing multiple candidates, it is easy for memories to become less clear. It is therefore important to meet soon after each candidate visits, receive congregational input, and write down impressions, both good and bad. It also gives you the opportunity to see all three of these men and their families in a similar setting to assess how well they may fit into your group.

The disadvantage of bringing in multiple candidates for try-outs is that you are bound to get differences of opinion. If you end up with a 50%, 30%, 20% split over the three men and hire the 50% "winner," you now have the other 50% of the congregation who did not choose the man who is hired. It opens the door for future complaints.

• **Option 2** requires your elders or search committee to rank the final three candidates based on what you've discovered about them through telephone interviews, reference checks, congregational visits, etc. If a clear ranking can be agreed upon, then set up the visit for your top candidate only. If he and his family make the impression you were hoping for, begin talks to hire him. If you aren't sure about him after the visit or if you were unable to agree on the terms for hiring him, you can then call in your second candidate and continue the same process with him. The advantage of doing it this way is that you avoid the "preacher parade" which most preachers hate. You also get your top candidate lined up for the "try out" first. This option requires that your elders or search committee worked hard to get to know the candidate prior to bringing him before the church.

A disadvantage of Option 2 is that the membership might feel that they weren't given any options. It is of the utmost importance that the congregation know and respect the search committee members who are making these decisions. They should also fully understand the process and the diligence that has gone into bringing this candidate before the congregation. If the congregation is provided with ample informal, personal time with the candidate as well as hearing him teach and preach, they should be able to either confirm or reject the committee's recommendation.

Step Eleven

Regardless of which option you choose from Step Ten, take the time to assess the applicants who have come to visit you. Review any feedback you have received. List the positive and negatives of having this person come and work with you. Lord willing, because you have immersed this entire process in prayer and done your homework, you'll have the best match possible. Usually search committees will go through this procedure and recommend a candidate to the eldership for final approval. Don't allow this final evaluation process to drag out. The applicant and his family are putting their lives on hold while they await your final answer. Do them the courtesy of making a decision within a couple of weeks of the last interview. Remember that each candidate, even the ones you decide are not right for your congregation, is a fellow brother in Christ. Treat him and his family with the dignity and respect with which you would like to be treated.

Step Twelve

It is now time for the eldership or leadership to make a decision as to whom they want to invite to come and work with them. Finalize a salary and compensation package that reflects the applicant's education and work experience. When considering compensation, don't forget to include at least a cost of living increase to his salary every year, as well as carving out time for him to refresh in order to prevent him from burning out. My current work agreement states that I can have four days off a year for personal enrichment and one quarter off from teaching. The personal enrichment gives me time to attend workshops or lectureships that help me improve my skills. A quarter off from teaching not only gives me a break, but allows others to develop their talents rather than always depending on the preacher to do it all. Many congregations pay for or supplement health insurance. Also, consider a retirement package. Harding University offers a 403(b) Retirement Plan that churches and ministers can participate in.

When making your offer, allow the applicant a couple of days to talk it over with his wife and pray about it before getting back to you. Understand he may have a work agreement that requires him to give anywhere from a two-week to a ninety-day notice. After one of your candidates has accepted your offer, inform the others of this decision immediately.

A Final Word

Taking more deliberate steps in searching for your next minister will help you to have a more successful search. Typically, it is expected that the congregation will cover traveling expenses, provide the family a place to stay during their visit, and pay the speaker an honorarium. Making a good impression on him and his family will go a long way toward sealing the deal. Understand that this is a stressful event for him and his family to have to go through because they are going into an unknown environment and worried about making a good impression on you as you are on them.

Again, I'm not expecting anyone to follow all of my recommendations. The Bible provides no specific guidelines for this process. I merely pray that the preceding ideas will spark discussions on how we can search for our ministers in a more planned and considerate way. It is my hope that if we do this, we'll all have to search a whole lot less often and be able to spend our time more productively serving God.

May the grace, peace, and wisdom of our Lord and Savior be with you all.

Reproducible Checklist

- **Phase One:** The leadership works among itself and with the congregation to address any problems related to the last minister leaving.
- **Phase Two:** Determine the congregation's profile and in which direction you want the church to move.
- **Phase Three:** Develop the ideal candidate profile and write out a job description of what you expect him to do for you and what you will do for him.
- **Phase Four:** Determine the search process.
  - **Step 1** Search Committee or Elders
  - **Step 2** What information do you want from your applicant?
  - **Step 3** How do you want to advertise your opening?
  - **Step 4** How long you will accept applications?
  - **Step 5** How will applications be handled as they come in and who will be responsible for processing them?
  - **Step 6** Apply candidate profile to applicants and eliminate any that do not meet the requirements.
  - **Step 7** Conduct phone interviews.
  - **Step 8** Reduce your list to top candidates and check references and job histories.
  - **Step 9** Determine a schedule of activities and meetings for your applicant(s) visit.

- ❏ **Step 10** Invite applicant(s) to visit your congregation.
- ❏ **Step 11** Assess the applicants in a timely manner.
- ❏ **Step 12** Make a final decision and finalize salary and compensation package.

SAMPLE JOB POSTING

Associate Minister Position

The Avenue Church of Christ is seeking a full-time Associate Minister. This minister oversees the day to day administrative functions of office supervision. He will be intimately involved in managing the education and small group program of the church. He will also be available to assist other ministries. The minister will collaborate with our active deacons and work closely with our shepherds as we implement our vision and ministries.

The congregation currently has 360 members, 5 shepherds, 2 full-time ministers, and office staff.

Bachelor's degree preferred in a ministry-related field.

Qualifications and Duties

Applicants will meet the following qualifications:

- Be a faithful, Christ-centered man, with a servant heart
- Have a successful history with church and administrative experience
- Have a teambuilding and collaborative style
- Be adept working with a diverse congregation and leadership team
- Be outgoing, people focused, and relationship driven
- Have excellent communicative skills
- Be organized, detailed, and purpose driven

Applicants will be familiar the following "key duties" (not an all-inclusive list):

- Collaboratively lead team of ministers in fulfilling church vision, goals, and direction
- Collaborate with deacons in fulfilling church vision, goals, and direction
- Work closely with shepherds in developing and implementing vision, goals, and ministries
- Serve as organizer for the education and small group program and work with respective deacons and ministries
- Initial contact for church related inquiries and needs, provide direction and guidance to appropriate ministries and leaders
- Occasional preaching or pulpit duties may be required
- Other ministry, business and administrative duties will be included
- Application Process
- Please email your application information to search@church.org by January 13, _____ (unless this date is extended).

    Please submit:
- A current, detailed resume
- A profile letter describing your experience, skills, leadership style, additional information relative to your qualifications, and why you desire this position.
- References that can be contacted during the evaluation phase.

The final applicant(s) must complete a background check on criminal history, driving records, and related employment records. A consumer credit report concerning credit standing, credit worthiness, and credit capacity will be completed.

Selection Process

The Search Committee will contact you if any additional information is needed. We will post any changes to the process or the following dates (estimated) on this website.

Timeline:

- Applications submitted through January 13
- Initial screening and telephone interviews as needed, through February 10
- Second screening, telephone interviews, and final candidate list through February 24
- Interviews through March 24
- Hiring by April 15

Additional Information

Any changes to this position will be posted on this webpage, so please check back often.

Please email questions or comments to Search Committee at search@church.org

SAMPLE INTERVIEW QUESTIONS

1. Tell us about your faith journey.
2. In general, what do you think your role should be?
3. Why are you interested in leaving your present position?
4. How long do you think you should stay and work with this congregation?
5. Will you be able to participate in camp, prison ministry, or visitation ministry?
6. How would you define success?
7. Please explain your understanding of the inspiration of the Bible.
8. What translation of the Bible do you prefer to use and why?
9. We have serious concerns about certain topics, issues, and doctrines that are currently being debated within our brotherhood. Please tell us your views of _____ .
10. How would you handle a situation in which you disagreed with a decision that the leadership made?
11. How would you handle a situation in which a member comes to you to complain about or criticize the leadership?
12. How do you see yourself fitting into the congregational leadership picture?
13. How would you help develop additional leaders?
14. In what ways do you feel you could you help this congregation grow?
15. What is your current schedule for teaching in the Sunday school and mid-week Bible programs? In your opinion, what would be the ideal situation?
16. What are your professional goals, short range and long range?

17. What hobbies or interests do you have that help you relax?
18. How do you typically respond to challenges presented by the leadership?
19. Our congregation has a long history of involvement with _____
20. (Bible camps, prison ministry, mission effort, visitation ministry, etc.). How does this ministry match your interests, skills, and experience?
21. What would you consider your greatest strengths?
22. What would you consider your greatest weaknesses?
23. What experience have you had in using software to enhance sermon presentation?
24. How do you see your role within the community?
25. What benefits would you expect us to provide for you and your family?
26. Take us through your normal work week schedule.
27. How many gospel meetings, workshops, or special classes would you expect to do each year?
28. What role will your wife play in your ministry? With the church?
29. Are there special accommodations needed in order for you to fulfill your responsibilities?
30. If selected for this position, how soon would you be able to start?
31. Other questions

For a free editable copy of this interview form go to www.21stcc.com and click on "Downloads."

SAMPLE WORK AGREEMENT

General Philosophy

_____ shall provide an energetic, Christ-like ministry to and in behalf of the local congregation in keeping with the church's mission, values, and goals. He will work closely with the leadership (elders and deacons) in promoting a positive environment for spiritual development and growth. He is to base his ministry on the application of biblical principles. He is to teach people patiently and correctly with gentleness, as well as to pursue righteousness, godliness, faith, love and endurance. Purity is a necessity as he is to be an example in speech and conduct. He must present the Word of God in honesty and truthfulness. He should help strengthen the faith of Christians, refute false teaching, and train others to carry on the work of the church.

Responsibilities

- Weekly sermon presentations
- Teach Sunday and Wednesday Bible classes for three quarters
- Positive interaction with the community and the lost
- Conduct personal Bible studies as requested
- Visitation to homes, hospitals, nursing homes
- Leadership training
- Lead/teach small groups
- Available for funerals and weddings
- Participation in local Bible camp as a teacher, chapel speaker, or counselor
- Maintain regular published office hours
- Be available for consultation or counseling for members
- Spend time in prayer for our nation, state, community, and congregation
- Participation in other ministries or activities hosted by the congregation
- The minister is encouraged to continue his education as long as the courses benefit his spiritual growth and are applicable to the local church. This education shall not conflict with his ability or time to perform his duties.

Pay and Benefits

- A yearly rate of _____ shall be paid on the first day of week. (Consider doing an annual review and giving at least a cost of living increase).
- A reimbursement allowance for auto, travel, and professional expenses considered ordinary and necessary for him to carry out his duties shall be fixed at _____.*
- A housing allowance of _____ shall be designated as a part of his living expenses.[1]
- Personal Time Off shall be arranged as following:
    ◊ 2 weeks vacation for 1 to 3 years of service
    ◊ 3 weeks vacation for 4 to 8 years of service
    ◊ 4 weeks vacation for 9+ years of service
- An allowance of $ _____ for one workshop away for personal enrichment (4 days).
- A limit of two gospel meetings or workshops to be conducted away each year.
- Paid holidays include the following: New Year's Day, Memorial Day, Independence Day, Labor Day, Thanksgiving Day, Christmas Eve, and Christmas Day. If a holiday falls on a Sunday it can be used the following Monday.

---

[1] Please check with local, state and federal guidelines to make sure you are in compliance with current statutes.

- One quarter off from teaching each year.
- Health insurance will be provided for the family.
- The congregation will contribute to a retirement plan of the minister's choosing.

<u>Termination</u>

Either party will give a thirty day written notice to the other if either party believes that the termination of the ministry is necessary.

Minister:_____   Elders:_____
                                                    _____
                                                    _____
                                                    _____
                                                    _____

www.ingramcontent.com/pod-product-compliance
Lightning Source LLC
Chambersburg PA
CBHW071414040426
42444CB00009B/2243